God's Bountiful Blessings

By Pastor Cecil A. Thompson

GOD'S BOUNTIFUL BLESSINGS!

PUBLISHED BY
ECONO PUBLISHING, LLC
Kuna, Idaho 83634
E-mail: admin@econopublishing.com
Website: www.econopublishing.com

Table of Contents

ACKNOWLEDGEMENTS

I dislike acknowledgements for a personal reason. Many years ago an evangelist held a series of meetings at the church we were attending. (I was not the pastor). He had written a book and asked my wife Joyce to proof and type his manuscript. Joyce agreed and spent about 30 hours laboriously completing the task. After she finished, the evangelist took the manuscript to the wife of a businessman in the church to put in a copy machine and make copies.

At the evangelist's final service that week, he asked the businessman and his wife to stand. He showered them with praise for their contribution to his book, but said nothing about the hours of work Joyce had given. I must confess that I was grieved by his neglect.

I do not want to fall into that same trap of ingratitude therefore I want to express my heartfelt thanks and gratitude to each and every person who has helped make this book possible. First and foremost, I want to thank the Lord Jesus Christ who has been my personal Savior since I was a young boy. Without Him I would be nothing and could do nothing. Thank you, Lord!

As the Daily-E-Votional grew from dozens of subscribers to thousands, it was very evident that I could not do it on my own. In stepped Russ Hanson from ReachOne.com Internet Providers. There is no way this ministry could have progressed without his wonderful help. Over these many years, numerous faithful friends have helped proofread the Daily-E-Votionals.

Joyce, my wife and closest friend, was always there with her red pen to help correct any errors in my text. Then Alex Villeneuve from Coral Ridge Ministries in Florida volunteered to proof-read the copy. When a job change prevented her continuing, Alex introduced me to her co-worker, Cathy Baker.

I cannot say enough about the years that Cathy Baker has devoted in giving her time and talent to prevent my making too many glaring grammatical errors. Not only that, she has given many hours proofreading the formulation of this book.

Larry "Buck" Hunter is the man who has taken on the Herculean task of cover design, formatting and publishing this book. He has also added visual interest to it with the graphics and my family pictures.

There are others who have contributed their encouragement and financial support over the years. The kind words of inspiration and love have been more than I deserve, but they have been so much appreciated that mere words can never adequately convey my gratitude.

To all of you who prayerfully read any or all of these words, I want to sincerely express my thanks and appreciation.

DEDICATION - MY TRIBUTE

My Tribute to the Vital Part of My Life—
MY WIFE! JOYCE ELAINE

After all of these years, how can I begin to explain the love I shared with Joyce? I began to discover the meaning of love when we were young and full of life. As near as I can recall, it was Sunday, August 22, 1948, in Nampa, Idaho, when I first saw Joyce. Sunday school class was about to start, and as usual, I was sitting next to my lifelong friend, Jerry, when the door of that classroom opened and Joyce stepped in with her sister. She was wearing a white and yellow dress that set off her pitch black hair. At that moment it seemed like my heart stopped beating. I turned to Jerry and said, "She's the one!" I didn't even know what that meant, but I knew that with one look she had stolen my heart.

A few weeks later there was a potluck dinner for several families who had moved from Camas, Washington, to Nampa. With my heart in my throat, I asked Joyce if she would like to go with me. I was sure that someone with her beauty and class would never have eyes for a clod like me. Amazingly she said yes! Later I learned that when we left the house that evening, her mother commented, "Just look at those two babies!"

That was to be the opinion of almost everyone back then. At just fourteen years of age we appeared to be too young to know what love was, but we did! Nat King Cole had a hit song back then that became ours.

It seemed to perfectly express our situation: ***"They Try to Tell Us We're Too Young." IT BECAME OUR SONG. IT GOES LIKE THIS: "They try to tell us we're too young, too young to really be in love; they say that love's a word, a word we've only heard but can't begin to know the meaning of.***

And yet we're not too young to know, this love will last though years may go, and then some day they may recall, we were not too young at all."

Looking back from this vantage point, I am amazed that our parents allowed us to date. That flicker of tender teenage love only grew stronger through our high school years. Other classmates would date for a time and then part for a new romance. But all the while, good ole Cec and Joyce never parted.

I still remember the sweet times we spent sharing our dreams with each other. Contrary to many modern couples, we waited to consummate our love until after we were married.

Our wedding night was special in so many ways. It was blistering hot and our pastor was out of town, so a college professor performed the ceremony. A prankster made an attempt to steal the keys of the car taking us on our honeymoon, but the plot failed. Our driver had a duplicate key and away we went. Love prevailed. We were now beginning our wonderful new life as husband and wife.

Within a few months I enlisted in the Air Force and we experienced our first taste of military life. It gave us an opportunity to see places and meet people who became dear friends.

It was during our assignment in Rapid City, South Dakota that our dear Brenda was born. Brenda died on July 11, 1991. Joyce died January 13, 2015. Oh, how I long to see her and Joyce once again. The next time will be in eternity and there will be no sorrow, pain, or separation.

I will see them healthy and happy beyond imagination. Our next two children, Dan and Lori, were both born in Nampa, Idaho. They have been such source of joy to me. Even in the trials of life they have shown love and respect and have always commented about the love they saw in their parents.

I am not sure when Joyce and me crossed the line from being young people to middle age people, to mature people, to elderly people, but in every age we have passed through, we have loved each other completely.

Sensual love is something that novelists have tried to portray, but our love has been far deeper. During the darkest days of trial and testing, we have known the love of Jesus and the love of each other.

We have shed our tears at the passing of our precious Brenda and then through the transplant surgeries of our dear Lori. What a gift of love from Brenda's daughter and our granddaughter, Jenna, who gave one of her kidneys to her aunt Lori. (That is keeping it in the family.)

Not only have we shared our love for each other, we have felt that love surround us. We thank everyone for their love.

Across these years I have seen the beautiful woman I first saw as a fourteen-year-old beauty who captured my heart on a Sunday morning, grow more and more feeble. But her beauty and loveliness has never faded from my sight.

They say that your memory is going to gradually recede as you grow older. But with my precious Joyce it was slipping far too rapidly. Many of her comments were just a little out of context. The doctors confirmed that she was suffering from dementia with Lewy bodies. We had never even heard of such an ailment before, but were now living with it.

In her last few months, I knew that we were losing her. Many times I would awaken and just gaze at her as she slept. When she was placed on hospice a hospital bed was set up in the living room. I would set beside her bed I look over the face of the gorgeous woman who has been beside me these many years.

We both knew the time was running out. In our quiet moments we tried to share just how precious we had been to each other. Not long ago Joyce paid me the highest honor a wife could give a husband when she said, ***"Honey, you are love personified!"*** I will always be that for you, Dear One. **I LOVE YOU DEARLY!** Wait for me Honey I still have work to do here on earth. I dedicate this book to you!

Your Devoted Husband, Cec

INTRODUCTION

GOD'S BOUNTIFUL BLESSINGS

I once heard the story of a beloved former pastor who was invited to preach at the church he had pastored for so many years. Many people who had been there under his ministry returned from some considerable distance to hear this precious saint of God proclaim from God's word one last time.

When he was introduced he slowly and very long laboriously shuffled to the pulpit. The congregation knew that this was likely to be the last time he would ever stand before a congregation. They leaned forward to strain and here those words that they once heard as he opened up the word of God and it became a life to them.

Many wondered what Scripture he would use or what outline he would present to highlight some special passage of Scripture. The crowd grew silent in the expectation.

In that poignant moment of time this precious pastor uttered these words; *"Jesus loves me, this I know, for the Bible tells me so!"* The congregation recognized this as a children's song, but now it became a life message from a dear saint of God.

Sometimes the simple spiritual truths are the most profound. Even hearing this story it seemed as though I was present in that congregation. I could sense, in fact I sense it right now, the depth of simple spiritual truth.

There is another story that almost parallels the one of the former pastor. It was of a young boy who had to memorize Psalm 23 and recite in front of his class. It was hard for him to memorize but he committed himself to constant reading and reciting. Even when he woke up at night he tried to recite it; *"The Lord is my Shepherd, I shall lack nothing!"* He was able to quote the entire chapter, beginning with this first sentence.

The day came for him to stand in front of his class and recite Psalm 23. It was at that time that stage fright took control. His mind was as blank as the blackboard that was behind him. Try as he might the words just became blurred. He finally was able to stammer out one statement; ***"The Lord is my Shepherd, that's all I need to know!"*** His class roared with glee at his embarrassment.

As I heard this story the thought that came into my mind was that he had it right! In fact if the psalmist David were standing beside him and uttered these

Words, I think he might've leaned down and whispered in that little boy's ear; ***"You know son, I think you have it right! He is our Shepherd and that is all we need to know!"***

If you read this book expecting something deep and theological you will be in for a big disappointment. There are fantastic Bible teachers who are able to do such research that it amazes. But I'm not one of those. I'm a very simple man who likes to keep things simple. I have blundered through life and enjoy every moment of it!

God's Bountiful Blessings will be my attempt to present the storehouse of God's blessing in a way that is in story form. There are some stories that I feel have strayed a little off of what is presented in the Bible. And where I find that, I will offer my own interpretation. I hope you find it truly God's Bountiful Blessing!

COUNT YOUR BLESSINGS.
NAME THEM ONE BY ONE.
COUNT YOUR
MANY BLESSINGS
SEE WHAT GOD HAS DONE.

ZACCHAEUS

Many times when we hear preaching or teaching from the Bible, it seems that it is not really looking at the Bible itself, so much as repeating what has been said about a particular passage before.

Let me give you an example: in Luke chapter 19, Jesus was passing through Jericho on His way to Jerusalem and eventually the cross, He encountered a man by the name of Zacchaeus. We're told that Zacchaeus was a man small in stature and also a chief tax collector. You know what people always think about tax collectors!

Zacchaeus wanted to see Jesus but he knew that his small stature prevented him from seeing over the crowd. Ignoring his prestige he tucked his robe around him and ran ahead of the procession. He then climbed a tree where he would be able to see Jesus.

The story is going pretty much the way we remember it right?

Jesus looks up to see Zacchaeus, calls him by name and says that He is going to his house for a meal. This did not sit well with the religious leaders of that area. How could a man of spiritual prominence like Jesus stoop to enter the house and have a meal with a mirror tax collector, one of the worst of sinners!

While at the house, Zacchaeus makes a startling statement. Let me quote it for you: ***"Look, Lord! Here and now I give half of my possessions to the poor, and if I have cheated anybody out of anything, I will pay back four times the amount."***

Are you following me to this point? This conniving, underhanded, cheating tax collector should not have had anyone of any spiritual significance in his home much less the son of God. Right?!

Now I have never been good at math. I wish I was, in fact I think it was because I had started school before I was really ready to learn and was always behind the power curve. But lacking a great ability in math I'd like us to look at something.

Let us say that Zacchaeus had a bank account of $10,000. He tells Jesus that he is going to give half of that to the poor, right? What does that leave? If my dumbbell math serves me well that means now he only possesses $5000. He then amazes me by saying that if he has cheated anyone out of <u>anything</u> he will pay back four times the amount.

If he had cheated in anyone by any means anyone, and paid back four times what he had cheated them out of, he could've been a destitute man. I think it speaks volumes that he was a man of integrity.

I really believe this was a testimony of a man who was honest. Yes he was a chief tax collector, but he took only what was required without receiving kickbacks of any sort.

We're not told what happened to Zacchaeus, but I do not think it's unreasonable to feel that he followed Jesus to Jerusalem. Jesus said that salvation had come to his house that day and I think from that moment on we can say that Zacchaeus was a follower of Jesus. I can almost see him in the crowd at the foot of the cross weeping openly.

If Jesus stopped by your house today and looked into your eyes what would He see? If you knew that you could hide nothing what would you be willing to commit yourself to? Zacchaeus committed himself to honest financial dealings and Jesus seeing his heart said that salvation had come. What would He see in your heart?

HAPPY BIRTHDAY!

How old are you? Well if you are under 9 you might answer 5 ½ or 8 ½. At that age you are always looking forward to the next birthday. I think as we grow older our responses change. We are almost 16, almost 19 and so on. At my age things are a lot different. I made it to 70, in my case I made it to 81. I think you get the point.

Stop and think for a moment with me about birthdays in the Bible. As near as I can tell in my study there are only two birthdays mentioned. By the way, one of those is not the birth of Jesus. We will get to that a little later.

The first birthday mentioned in the Bible is in the book of Genesis. It was the birthday of Pharaoh. You may recall that Joseph was in prison and two of Pharaoh's subordinates were sent to prison. One was the Cupbearer the other was the Baker.

These two men had dreams and Joseph was able to interpret the dreams. He told them that in three days they would be released from prison. The Cupbearer would be returned to its original position serving Pharaoh.

This really excited the Baker and he was anticipating a favorable interpretation of his dream. Unfortunately there was not a favorable interpretation for him. In three days he was to be beheaded and his body impaled on a pole. These interpretations were fulfilled to the letter.

So the first birthday mentioned in Scripture ended with a beheading. Not a very exciting way to spend a birthday is it?!

The second birthday we read about is in the New Testament. It was the birthday of King Herod. John the Baptist had been extremely critical of Herod because he had taken his brother, Philip's wife, Herodias as his own wife. Herod had arrested John and placed him in prison.

At his birthday celebration the daughter of Herodias, Salome danced for Herod. He foolishly promised her anything she wanted and at the prompting of her mother, Herodias asked for John's head on a platter. Herod had John beheaded and so on the only other birthday recorded in Scripture there was another beheading.

So what about the birthday of Jesus? Was He really born on December 25th? Well we don't know for sure.

There is some doubt that this was the date of His birth. There is some doubt that shepherds would be in the fields with their flocks toward the end of December.

I have read some Bible scholars who conjecture that more probably this was about the time of his immaculate conception. That being the case it's more likely that He was born in the fall rather than late winter.

The date of Jesus' birth may be in question, but the important thing is that Jesus **was born**. He actually left the glory of heaven to be born as a helpless baby in Bethlehem. Wow! I hope that resonates with you as it does with me. His birth was supernatural and God became man and dwelt here on earth. The date is not important, but His having been born to provide eternal salvation is of supreme importance.

"And she brought forth her firstborn Son, and wrapped Him in swaddling clothes, and laid Him in a manger, because there was no room for them in the inn." Luke 2:7

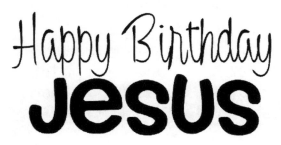

DEALING WITH PRIDE

It's Not Me – It's The Lord

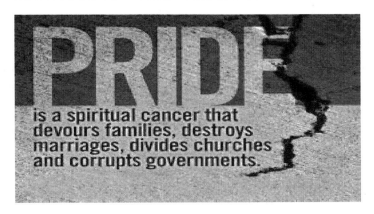

PRIDE is a spiritual cancer that devours families, destroys marriages, divides churches and corrupts governments.

Pride is an ugly thing. The very first sin recorded in the Bible was the sin of pride when the serpent tempted Eve by saying that by eating the fruit of the knowledge of good and evil she would be like God. That is pride! By the way, we read that Adam was next to her and she handed the fruit to him as well, so to blame only Eve would be erroneous.

There are countless examples of spiritual pride recorded in God's word. One that stands out in my mind was that of Joseph. This was a young man who was favored by his father, favored by God, but despised by his brothers. They despised him so much that they wanted to kill him. Instead they sold him into slavery. It seemed as if God had lost control of the situation, but that is never the case. God is always in control.

Even though Joseph was elevated to a high position in the house of Potiphar, the man who had purchased him, he never forgot who his real master was. When tempted by Mrs. Potiphar he knew it would be a transgression against his God as well as her husband.

In Genesis 40:8, Joseph tells Pharaoh's cup bearer and baker that the interpretation of dreams belongs to God. You may recall that both of these interpretations proved to be true. The baker was executed and the cupbearer restored to his former position. He forgot the promise he made to Joseph for two years.

So what happens when a prisoner stands before the king or in this case Pharaoh? With fellow prisoners he said it was God who interpreted the dreams. But now he has the opportunity before the most powerful man in all of the land to take credit for interpretations. Would he allow pride to slip in and take credit? Not Joseph. In Chapter 41 we read that he tells Pharaoh that interpretation of dreams belongs to God. What a man!

In the book of Daniel we consistently see that Daniel was a man who trusted God completely. Since he was a prisoner and taken into exile there might've been room for resentment and bitterness, but there wasn't.

Nebuchadnezzar was a vicious tyrant. He had absolute and total control. He had a dream but could not remember what the dream was. He called for his magicians, enchanters, sorcerers and astrologers to come and tell him what his dream was and then give him the interpretation. Of course they could not do so and told him it was impossible for anyone to do such a thing. At that Nebuchadnezzar ordered all of the wise men and interpreters of dreams be put to death. That included Daniel.

Daniel stood before this violent king and even though he was able to tell Nebuchadnezzar the dream and its interpretation, he took no credit. Here is what he said to the king. ***"No wise man, enchanter, magician or diviner can explain to the king the mystery he has asked about, but there is a God in heaven who reveals mysteries. He has shown King Nebuchadnezzar what will happen in days to come."***

Isn't that fantastic?! These examples of humility reveal to us that we should always give God the glory and never take any credit ourselves. Like Daniel said, there is a God in heaven and He is the one who knows all things and controls all things.

The next time we are tempted to take credit for anything we have done remember Joseph. Remember Daniel. Remember the heroes of the faith who always gave the credit to God and never took it themselves.

May our response to praise always be?

IT'S NOT ME – IT'S THE LORD

HELLO BARNABAS!

"Joseph, a Levite from Cyprus, whom the apostles called Barnabas (which means "son of encouragement"), sold a field he owned and brought the money and put it at the apostles' feet."

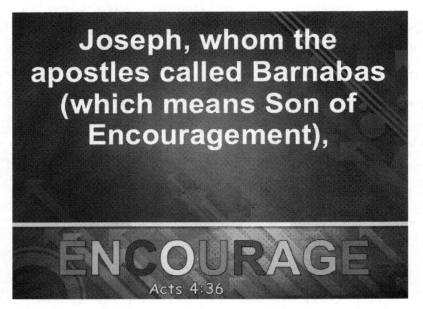

Years ago I spent several hours of Bible study on this man Barnabas. I had heard his name but I really did not have the feeling that I knew him. That was about to change! I think one of the reasons that I was interested in Barnabas was the parenthetical statement that Barnabas means the son of encouragement.

I feel that I have the gift of exhortation and encouragement. I wanted to see what type of character in Scripture I could relate to. I think I found it in Barnabas! Let me share with you some of the things that I found about this notable character.

First of all his real name was not Barnabas it was Joseph. When his mother held him for the first time, with his father hovering nearby, the name they gave to this small creature was Joseph. I love the name Joseph. I love the character Joseph. This tiny baby had a lot to live up to with a name like Joseph and he certainly did!

He lived up to it so completely that his name was changed and he was given a nickname, **Barnabas**. As mentioned a few moments ago he was an encourager. What type of a man would be called an encourager? Pure and simple it was someone who looked for and saw the good in people. That was Barnabas!

We also read in this Scripture that he was a Levite and he was from Cyprus. The tribe of Levi was assigned the responsibility of caring for the temple. In other words he had a spiritual responsibility. We are not told if Barnabas ever had official responsibilities in connection with being a Levite, but he certainly was a believer in the Lord Jesus Christ.

Cyprus is an island in the Mediterranean. At some time before we read about   Barnabas he left Cyprus and journeyed to Jerusalem. We are not told any of the details that led him to leave his home. I think one of the reasons...perhaps the primary reason, was because he was a man who sought after God.

The one thing that we do learn about Barnabas is that he was committed to finding God. In the process he found the son of God, Jesus! Someone who seeks after God is more interested in the things of God than in the worldly possessions they possess. Barnabas held ownership in a field of some type. He showed his faithfulness to God and the work of the church by selling that field and bringing the proceeds to the Apostles.

In addition to being a son of encouragement, as he was called, he had a generous spirit. He owned a piece of land which he sold in order to bring the proceeds to the apostles for the ministry of the church. After bringing his gift things go silent about this man Barnabas. We read that Ananias and Sapphira attempted to deceive the apostles by bringing only a portion of what they had sold, but saying they had brought all of the proceeds from the sale. (It resulted in their death).

We read nothing more about Barnabas until we come to chapter 9 in the book of acts. Saul, who was a vicious persecutor of Christians had been converted on the road to Damascus. In Damascus he became a target of the Jewish leaders and had to flee for his life. He made his way to Jerusalem to meet with the apostles. In Acts 9:26 and 27 Barnabas re-enters the picture:

"And when Saul had come to Jerusalem, he tried to join the disciples; but they were all

afraid of him, and did not believe that he was a disciple. <u>But Barnabas</u> took him and brought him to the apostles. And he declared to them how he had seen the Lord on the road, and that He had spoken to him, and how he had preached boldly at Damascus in the name of Jesus."

You'll notice that I have taken the liberty of underlining the words, "<u>But Barnabas</u>." Barnabas stands out as a person who had pertinent information about what had happened to Saul. How did he know this? I think he knew it because he was one who always looked for the good in people. He no doubt spoke with Christians from Damascus who told the story of what they knew about what had happened to Saul.

What was the result of his action? Well the result was that Saul was able to meet, speak, and spend time with the Apostles who had once been his enemies. I'm sure the Apostles were nervous at first, but they trusted Barnabas. Not only was he an encourager, but he was reliable. I wish we had more Barnabas like people today!

Later on in the book of Acts we read that spiritual opposition to Saul became so severe that he had to be secretly evacuated from Jerusalem. He returned to his original home in Tarsus.

But that was not the end for Saul and Barnabas played a huge part in what was going to happen to him. Word came to the church in Jerusalem that there was a group of believers meeting in Antioch.

They wanted to ensure that it was legitimate and who else did they send but dear old Barnabas! He determined that it was true that they truly were believers and in fact we read that the believers in Antioch were the first ones to be called Christians.

After sending his report back to Jerusalem Barnabas journeyed to Tarsus. He had one objective and that objective was to find Saul. I have no idea how large Tarsus was at the time, but I'm sure he immediately went to the district where the tentmakers plied their trade. He was able to find Saul and took him back to Antioch.

Let me quote from Acts 13:1-2; *"Now in the church that was at Antioch there were certain prophets and teachers: Barnabas, Simeon who was called Niger, Lucius of Cyrene, Manaen who had been brought up with Herod the tetrarch, and Saul. As they ministered to the Lord and fasted, the Holy Spirit said, 'Now separate to Me Barnabas and Saul for the work to which I have called them.'"*

For one entire year Barnabas ministered in Antioch. As you read these two verses you'll notice that Barnabas is mentioned first and Saul is mentioned last. We find support to believe that those with preeminence are always listed first and so on down the line. This might indicate that Saul was still in a learning phase.

The Holy Spirit called Barnabas and Saul to embark on a missionary journey. Their first stop was Cyprus.

Isn't that interesting since that was where Barnabas had come from. They were in a city called Paphos when they were confronted by a false prophet named Bar-Jesus. Saul confronted the man and by the power of the Holy Spirit pronounced blindness upon him. The significance is that at this moment we read that Saul's name was changed to Paul.

Almost from the moment that Saul became Paul, Barnabas assumed a supportive position. He never seemed to resent this new status. You see he was the son of encouragement. His task was to build up others, not himself.

We can read further in the book of Acts and see that this faithful servant of the Most High God was truly the son of encouragement! As I began writing about Barnabas I mentioned that one of my aims in studying his life was to apply it in my own life. My primary desire in life is to build others up by challenging and encouraging them to make Christ first in their life. I hope this study of Barnabas has done that for you.

EYE WITNESSES!

 I have been blessed to have filled many unique positions across the years of my life. One of the most interesting was when I served as a County Juvenile Probation Officer. It was a small County and I had the privilege of speaking with the judge during recesses. I was amazed as he would discuss with me the case that was being argued. He remarked; "I have no idea why they do not call witnesses who observed what had actually taken place."

2 Peter 1:16-18
16 we...were eyewitnesses of his majesty. 17 For he received from God the Father honour and glory, when there came such a voice to him from the excellent glory, This is my beloved Son, in whom I am well pleased.

I asked if he could make the decision anyway and he shook his head no. He explained that in a court of law a witness was necessary to substantiate the argument that was being presented. A witness could be someone who observed a crime taking place or testifying to some test that had been made.

Many times as I looked around the courtroom I observed that it was filled with spectators. They were observing what was taking place and the testimony that was being provided, and even though they were witnessing it they were not what could be considered witnesses. They were observers!

You may wonder why I make such a big deal of this. I think it's because we quite often get a wrong idea of a particular passage of Scripture. It is found in Hebrews chapter 11.

Let me give you a list of these heroes of the faith that were mentioned in Hebrews chapter 11; Abel, Enoch, Noah, Abraham, Isaac, Jacob, Sarah, Joseph, Moses, Rahab, Gideon, Barak, Sampson, Jephthah, David, Samuel, and the Prophets.

 Let me ask you a personal question. Have you ever visualized some that were on this list or others who have died and gone to be with the Lord, looking down at everything you did? Have you thought of them as witnesses against you? I wish I could hear your answers. If I could I'm sure you would say that you have felt that way.

Sometimes we have a distorted view of heaven. We speak people who have gone to be with the Lord looking down on us. Watching what we do. Somehow giving us encouragement because they see what we are doing.

Now if there are no tears in heaven, which is what we are told, would there be tears in their eyes when see the things we are doing down here? Now maybe you are perfect but I want to tell you I'm not. I personally think that those who have gone to be with the Lord have their eyes so filled with his glory and the magnificence of heaven that there's no time to be looking back at the things of this world.

So what about those witnesses? If they are not staring at us and everything we do, what are they witnessing to? What does God want us to learn from them? Each of them demonstrated faith. Let us briefly recall what qualifies them for God's Hall of Faith.

ABEL: He brought the best of his flocks as a sacrifice to God. His brother Cain took the low road approach and brought only some of the produce from his fields. It certainly spoke of Abel bringing a blood sacrifice which was pleasing to God. There are still those today who try to approach God on the basis of their own works rather than on the shed blood of Jesus Christ. Abel became the charter member and God's Hall of Fame

ENOCH: He pleased God and walked with God. What a beautiful picture comes into my mind when I think of the intimate fellowship that Enoch had with God. He walked with Him and talked with Him. He demonstrated faith which pleased God and God took him home to heaven without experiencing death.

NOAH: When God told Noah to build an ark since He was going to send a flood upon the earth, he had faith that what God said, God would do. That was faith and he and his family were saved when the waters rose and destroyed the earth.

ABRAHAM: What a man of faith Abraham was! Out of the clear blue God appeared to him and called him to go to a land that would be his inheritance. He was told to go but he was not told where it was he was going. He had to have faith and trust that the God who called him would be the same God who would him. That my friend requires faith! And that is one of the things that he is commended for.

It's interesting to note that he lived his entire as a stranger in a foreign country. But here is where the real vision of faith appears. It says in Hebrews eleven verse ten that he was looking for a city without foundations, whose architect and builder is God. What magnificent faith he demonstrated.

Abraham was also commended for his faith in believing God who promised him that he would be the father of a multitude. In fact we are told that his descendants would be as numerous as the stars in the sky and the sand on the seashore. Problem! He had no children but as a man of almost 100 with a wife past 90 God fulfilled the promise to this man of faith.

That is not the end for Abraham, for God had more work for him to do. It was not an easy task, it required more faith than perhaps Abraham had ever been called upon to demonstrate. God called him to sacrifice his own son.

By faith he obeyed God and was called to the very spot that centuries later God's own dear son was sacrificed. God provided a ram at just the right moment. How could he do that? It says here in Hebrews eleven verse nineteen that Abraham reasoned that God could grades Isaac from the dead, and figuratively he did. Abraham's faith was rewarded!

ISAAC: The power of blessing is demonstrated in the life of Isaac. By faith he gave a blessing to his two sons Jacob and Esau. Sometimes when we pronounce a blessing on a person we take it lightly. If Isaac could be commended for his faith in giving a blessing, we need to take seriously our responsibility to bless others.

JACOB: The faith that Isaac demonstrated in pronouncing blessing was repeated by his son Jacob. He blessed the two sons of Joseph and worshiped the God who had been so faithful to him across the years of his life.

JOSEPH: The life of Joseph was a constant demonstration of faith. While he was favored by his father, his real confidence came from his relationship with God. He consistently lived his life depending upon his God. In faith he saw the time when his family and nation would return to Israel. His request was that his bones be returned to the land of his ancestors. By faith he believed!

MOSES: Moses was commended for his faith in numerous ways. Even though he was raised in Pharaoh's own household he chose to endure the sufferings of his own people rather than enjoy the pleasures of sin for a season. Walking away from a life of ease he experienced years of tedious labor as a shepherd in Midian.

When God called him to return to Egypt and lead his people Moses new it was a difficult if not humanly impossible situation, but by faith he believed God rather than human reasoning. That took faith! He stood toe to toe with Pharaoh and pronounced God's judgments upon Pharaoh and the land.

By faith Moses believed God concerning the Passover and prepared his people to leave and possess the land that God had promised. He was consistently misunderstood, criticized, and condemned, yet by faith he remained true to God. There was one outburst in which he acted in anger rather than obedience but still is commended as a man of faith.

RAHAB: She was a harlot but turned from her sinful ways saved the lives of the two spies, the lives of her entire family, and eventually became a part of the lineage of David the king of Israel and eventually...Jesus. What faith!

GIDEON, BARAK, SAMSON, JEPHTHAH, DAVID, SAMUEL, and PROPHETS AND MANY OTHERS: There could never be enough words to describe the faith of those who have gone before us. They lived faithful lives and died victoriously. What a witness we have as we read of how their faith played out and the glory of the Lord enveloped them.

We are called to witness these lives. Having been given that example, we need to live our lives in such a manner that those who follow in her footsteps will be able to witness our total dependence upon God!

FATEFUL BUT FAITHFUL DANIEL!

When you are born into royalty it may seem that you have it made. You will not have the ongoing task of living hand to mouth. Unfortunately that is not always the case. As a matter of fact living in the days of Daniel, to be born into royalty was to face constant danger of losing life or limb.

The northern kingdom of Israel had consistently turned their back on God and as a result had gone into exile many years before Daniel. It would certainly seem that the southern kingdom of Judah would learn a lesson from what had happened to Israel. Just like us that did not happen. King after king would depart from the obedient worship of the God who had been so faithful to them.

Let me interject that there were a few kings that were faithful, but more and more they went their own willful way instead of trusting in God. It seems unfair that the children have to suffer for the sinful ways of their fathers, but that is what happened to Daniel and others with him.

If we were to open up the book of Daniel, immediately we would find that Daniel and three of his friends especially are mentioned here. They were part of the royal family from Judah who had been exiled by King Nebuchadnezzar and hauled off too far away Babylon.

Here is where fate steps in and faith is a choice. What happens when the young men of royal blood are taken into captivity? Well there is a prophecy that gives us a very strong suggestion. Let me quote it for you from Isaiah 39:7; *"And they shall take away some of your sons who will descend from you, whom you will beget; and they shall be eunuchs in the palace of the king of Babylon."* Those were the words of prophecy given by Isaiah to Hezekiah, King of Judah.

So we ask ourselves the question: "was this prophecy fulfilled?" Perhaps we have our answer in the book of Daniel itself. In Daniel 1:6-7 we read these words; *"Now from among those of the sons of Judah were Daniel, Hananiah, Mishael, and Azariah. To them the chief of the eunuchs gave names: he gave Daniel the name Belteshazzar; to Hananiah, Shadrach; to Mishael, Meshach; and to Azariah, Abed-Nego."*

It is interesting to note that it was the chief of eunuchs who gave the names to Daniel and his three companions.

We like to think good thoughts about those who are faithful to God. Fact of the matter is that God has allowed, and still allows His children to go through the most extenuating circumstances. While Scripture does not plainly state that Daniel and his three friends were made eunuchs it certainly seems likely that they were. A violent King like Nebuchadnezzar did not want royalty from any nation that was subjected by him to produce lineage that might contaminate his own bloodline.

As I often meditate upon the sin of the northern kingdom of Israel and a southern kingdom Judah, I think of the way they had neglected God ,turned away from him completely, and now were paying the price for their rejection of the Lord God who had delivered them from the bondage of Egypt.

It is far too easy to lump the sins of a nation with the behavior of individuals within that nation. While Daniel, Shadrach, Meshach, and Abednego were part of a sinful nation that was carried away into exile, they demonstrated a faithfulness to God that is a living example to anyone who reads God's word. Instead of becoming bitter they became better.

You may recall that Nebuchadnezzar had a disturbing dream. The problem was he could not remember what the dream was, therefore there was no way to interpret the meaning of the dream. All of the wise men in his kingdom were not able to do the impossible... Tell him the dream he had and then interpret it. This evil king was so unreasonable that he ordered that all wise men in the kingdom be executed and that included Daniel and his friends.

What would you do if you were faced with an impossible situation? That is exactly what Daniel was confronted with. I honestly do not think that Daniel was so fearful for his own life that he begged to be spared, rather I think he knew that there was a God in heaven who had something in store for Nebuchadnezzar that neither Daniel nor the king himself could even imagine.

Daniel was, by the way, able to call upon God and perform the impossible. Why? Because even though he found himself in a <u>fateful</u> situation he was <u>faithful</u> in that situation. He let the King know that it was not his doing but God himself who gave the dream and the interpretation.

When we read about the three Hebrew children who refused to bow down and worship the huge image that Nebuchadnezzar had erected. By the way this huge image was some 90 feet tall and 9 feet wide. You may recall the story that the three Hebrews, Shadrach, Meshach, and Abednego refused to bow down and were cast into the fiery furnace. They were not harmed in any way and when Nebuchadnezzar looked inside he saw not three, but four people. Very possibly the fourth was the pre-incarnate appearance of Jesus.

But where was Daniel? Very possibly because of telling Nebuchadnezzar his dream and then interpreting the dream he was promoted and was about his duties at the time of the fiery furnace incident.

This faithful servant of God never allowed the painful circumstances of his life to get his eyes off of the Lord. Years later when fellow administrators became jealous of Daniel, they tried to find some fault that would bring about his fall. He was surrounded by many observers who were prepared to scrutinize the most intimate details of his life that would bring about his fall.

In Daniel 6:5 we read these words; *"We shall not find any charge against this Daniel unless we find it against him concerning the law of his God."* I wonder if we were surrounded by a host of witnesses who were trying to find some charge against us, would they conclude the same thing as these men did about Daniel.

This is just a very brief look into the life of a man who no doubt was emasculated, and yet was so faithful that he never took his eyes off of God. He became God's instrument to touch wicked Kings with the power of God unto salvation.

In 1958 when our son was born, Joyce and I labored to come up with a name for our newborn son. Our desire was for him to become a strong man of God who would be willing to stand up in the face of opposition. And so we named him Daniel. Over these many years our son has demonstrated many of the qualities that I have seen in the book of Daniel. He was named well!

> "IF WE WERE THROWN INTO THE BLAZING FURNACE, THE GOD WHOM WE SERVE IS ABLE TO SAVE US. HE WILL RESCUE US FROM YOUR POWER, YOUR MAJESTY."
>
> SHADRACH, MESHACH AND ABEDNEGO TO NEBUCHADNEZZAR

HUSBANDS

Sometimes I am prone to think that men are a mess! That is especially true for husbands. In recent years it seems that men have this desire to have a man cave in their home. I'm not sure where it started or when it started, but it seems to be the latest fad. Personally I think it's the worst possible thing that a husband, a father or any man could do. It is like cutting out everybody else from their life and hibernating like some animal.

In over fifty years of counseling I have found that men have hurt their wives and children to a degree that it has wounded their spirits. In Colossians chapter three verse twenty-one, the apostle Paul takes aim at fathers. He warns fathers against provoking their children. He says that by provoking them you will discourage them and turn them away from the faith. I wonder how many children have been turned away from faith in the living God because of a father who provoke them to frustration.

During courtship many men behave themselves and treat their future wife with love and respect and dignity. After the marriage things have a tendency to change. Instead of devoting themselves to their wife and family they become self-centered and selfish, thinking only what will satisfy themselves.

So what is the example that husbands are to follow? And we have no need to look further than Ephesians chapter five versus twenty-five through twenty-eight: ***"Husbands, love your wives, just as Christ also loved the church and gave Himself for her, that He might sanctify and cleanse her with the washing of water by the word, that He might present her to Himself a glorious church, not having spot or wrinkle or any such thing, but that she should be holy and without blemish.***

So husbands ought to love their own wives as their own bodies; he who loves his wife loves himself."

I want to direct your attention especially to Christian husbands. How much do you love the Lord? If Jesus walked into the room right now and you walked toward Him as a born-again believer, how much would you tell Him you loved Him? What words would you use? What expression would be on your face as you gazed upon Him?

Now, with that in your mind go back and read this passage of Scripture from Ephesians. Do you see how Christ demonstrated his love to the church? He loved her (the church) with His arms stretched out on the cross. He demonstrated love by sacrificing Himself.

In my premarital counseling I make a point of challenging the man to give himself fully and completely for his wife. Not for the gratification it would bring him, but in obedience to God's word.

Want to tell you right now it has not always worked. Even though there was a promise made, many husbands failed to follow through on their promise. They became more and more distant and preoccupied with **things** rather than the most important **thing**, their wife.

Want to share with you something that happened in my own life. I had been faithfully studying God's word for many years. I realize that I had become protective of my own time and my own energy. I was more interested in how I felt than how my wife felt. Oh please understand I loved her with all my heart but I didn't show it fully.

I was extremely weary one late afternoon as I drove home from work. I prayed as I drove. Now I didn't kneel and I didn't close my eyes so please do not call the state police and report me. But I had a wonderful conversation with the Lord. I promised to begin dying to myself in order to show my love for my wife.

I think the Holy Spirit had intentionally caused frustrations and difficult situations that day in order to drain me physically and mentally. I could hardly wait to get home to finish dinner and stretch back in my recliner for a well-earned rest. The Lord said **"NO!"** Immediately I knew that my job that evening was to take the pressure off my wife and do more than I had ever done.

After dinner I took her in the living room, set her down in a recliner and told her I was taking

Page | 41

responsibility for the kitchen. I cleared the dishes, ran the water in the sink with the soap and begin to scrub away. I recall looking out the window above the sink and feeling the fatigue sweep over me. In that moment of time, as simple as it was, I knew there was a turning point in my life and tears began to roll down my cheeks.

When I finished with the dishes I went into the living room and knelt down beside the chair where Joyce was reclining. I told her how much I loved her and how special she was to me. I told her that it wasn't enough just to **say** the words "I love you" but I wanted to **demonstrate** how much I loved her. Then we both began to cry. Our love had always been very deep, but that evening it increased tenfold.

That was not the end, it was just the beginning. I began to find the ultimate joy in being the husband that God intended me to be. Not only was I committed to love my wife in the same way that Christ loved the church and gave himself for her, I also realize that it was important that I protect her, so that others would never see any weakness that she might have.

Our relationship was like a conspiracy. We took care to cover each other's faults. I think I had more to cover than she did! But we found joy in it. Toward the end of her life there is very little that she could do. Because I had demonstrated my love in so many different ways, it made it easier for her to accept allowing me to do things that otherwise would have been embarrassing. It only drew us closer.

One of the highest compliments I have ever received from anyone in all of my life came from my wife. I do not remember exactly what precipitated her comment but it stunned me and brought me to tears. Joyce looked at me with endearing eyes and said; "Honey, you are love personified!" The last night of her life it was not possible for her to take her medicine. I had to grind it up I fed it to her using a baby spoon. I will always remember her sweet smile.

HUSBANDS, love your wives, even as Christ also loved the church, and gave himself for it.

– EPHESIANS 5:25

WIVES

"Wives, submit to your own husbands, as to the Lord. For the husband is head of the wife, as also Christ is head of the church; and He is the Savior of the body. Therefore, just as the church is subject to Christ, so let the wives be to their own husbands in everything."

These verses from Ephesians chapter five have been used and misunderstood for many years. Many men are quick to take those first words and demand that their wives submit to every command they give them. This has led to bitter arguments and even divorce. How terribly sad that is!

The word submit is the Greek word, *hypotassō*. It has an interesting meaning. It means to come under the authority of another. Not only that but it has the implication of voluntarily coming under the authority of one who is placed in charge.

Having spent more than twelve years in the military I understand the necessity of a chain of command. I was in the Air Force and therefore came in contact with many pilots. I even flew on aircraft controlled by the pilot. The pilot was in ultimate control but many times he relied upon a navigator and other key personnel. Without their input disaster would almost be certain.

There is no question about the fact that God established the husband to be the head of the home. That does not mean he is smarter than or better than his wife. It is a position in which he is responsible under God to care for his family. Any time a wife tries to take control of the home she is coming out from under his God given protection and there is trouble ahead!

Now let me quickly explain that the husband is under the authority of God Himself. Any time he tries to take control of the situation without seeking the approval of God there is danger ahead. In fact he can pattern for his wife what it really means to be in subjection to the authority of another.

Years ago I was teaching a Sunday school class called Pairs and Spares. There were some married couples in the class, some single individuals, and a few who were engaged to be married. One of the engaged couples had a humorous dialogue going. He would tell her; "Submit woman!" She would just smile and say; "Die man!" She would then go on to explain the true role of a husband and wife. That couple has been married for many fruitful years.

It just came to my mind that I observed a beautiful relationship between husband and wife. It was while I served on the staff of a large church. One of our groups was planning a retreat at a lake north of Boise, Idaho. Joyce and I visited the facility a few months in advance to ensure that it would be adequate.

The husband and wife were showing us around the grounds and all of the amenities that would be provided. The wife was very outgoing and gregarious while the husband was very quiet and withdrawn. It met all of the requirements that we were looking for. We reserved the facilities immediately.

When the large group appeared for our retreat, the husband and wife went on a tour with the entire group just as they had done with just Joyce and me. Since I had been on the tour before I was able to set back and watch as the wife happily explained the Lord had opened the doors for this ministry and what they had to offer.

I was at the back of the room as the wife was speaking and could see her husband sitting on the back row as his wife spoke. It was then I noticed that from time to time he would nod or very gently shake his head. His motions were almost invisible, but I noticed his wife was reacting to them.

After the tour in the group had been dismissed I talked to her and her husband. I commented about what I had observed and mentioned that it appeared that she was a submissive wife, looking to her husband for his approval. She began to cry! She told me that many people felt that she was domineering and not submissive. It was not the case at all. It was easy for her to speak to people while her husband was very shy and withdrawn. They used their strong points to function as a united couple.

Wives are like love sponges! Many husbands fail to realize how important it is for them to tell their wives how much they love them and then demonstrate that love by giving themselves sacrificially to their wife. Love motivates a wife!

What many wives fail to understand is that husbands have a great need in their own life. Unlike a woman, a man needs honor and respect. Those two qualities are as important to a man as love is to a woman. I often encourage wives to be observant of things they can say and show that they honor and respect this man who is there husband. It might be small things to them, but whenever they tell their husbands that they respect them for what they have said or done, they give them honor. Keep your eyes open wives! At the beginning you might have to look closely to discover qualities that you can honestly say you respect and honor, but when you see them make sure you mention them to that husband of yours!

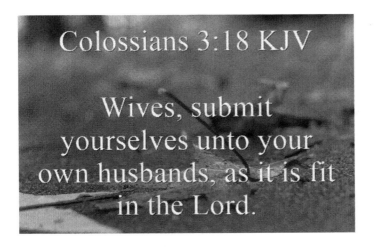

Colossians 3:18 KJV

Wives, submit yourselves unto your own husbands, as it is fit in the Lord.

TWO LOST SONS

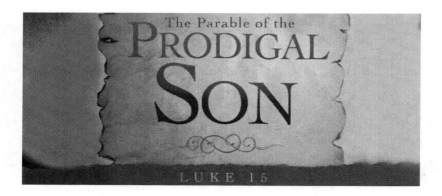

Day after day there was the same turmoil. A frustrated father was caught between the bitterness and argumentative attitude of his two sons. Try as he might there was no way he could stop the arguments and bitterness that caused chaos in the home.

The older son many times tried to act more like a father than a brother. Naturally this caused arguments and bitterness. The father felt like he was always called upon to be a referee between the two boys. Actually they were young men rather than young boys but the arguments had begun when they were just youngsters and continued into adulthood.

The younger son spent much of his time with his friends. He ignored the rules that his father had imposed but did his own thing. The long-suffering father felt as though his heart would break within him. He loved these two sons and wanted only the best for them.

You recognize I'm sure that this is a parable that that Jesus told. Many times we have called it the parable of the prodigal son. It's interesting to discover that the word prodigal is actually not mentioned. But the description is there regardless. In the Hebrew it means excessively wasteful. Do you know children like that? As a matter of fact do you have children like that? If you do you can sympathize with this father in the parable.

There came a day when the young son lashed out at his father in anger and asked for his portion of the inheritance. In that day the older son would have received a greater share, but the young son did not want to wait until the death of his father to receive the portion that would have come to him.

Perhaps it was because the father realized his two sons would not stop their angry attitude toward each other that he decided to give each their inheritance. That is a part of the parable that many times we overlook. Not only did the father give the younger son his portion of the inheritance, he also gave the older son his portion of the inheritance.

I'm sure it was a very sad picture the day the younger son walked away from the house carrying his earthly possessions along with the portion of the inheritance that had just been given to him. Rather than staying close by he went to a far country.

We are not told where that far country was, the only identifying thing is that it was a far country. That would indicate there would be no communication once the young son left. I can visualize the

Page | 49

brokenhearted father watching as his beloved son walked away from home with his few worldly possessions. As he finally disappeared from view the father continued to watch expectantly, waiting for his return.

I'm sure that both of his sons felt satisfied and happy. If we were to be able to read their minds I'm sure that they would feel like finally I don't have to put up with that other brother who has been a pain in my side for so long. I'm finally free of that irritation! While the brothers rejoiced the father wept.

When the young son finally came to the end of his journey he was soon surrounded by those who are eager to share along with him a riotous way of life. We are not told the details only that he wasted his inheritance on riotous living.

Meanwhile back at the ranch, as it were, the older still seethed with resentment. He was angry as he went about operating the family business. In his mind he had the picture of his younger brother wasting his life with harlots. Jesus never mentions that the younger brother did this, and since it was a far country to which the young son had gone there was no way that the older brother could have known what he was doing.

It makes me stop and realize that while the young son had left the father to go to a far country the older son had gone away from his father as well. His journey took him into the realm of bitter resentment and perhaps even jealousy. One son left physically and the other son left emotionally. But both sons seem to be lost to the father and his heart was heavy.

Sin does not usually bring about rational thinking. The younger son probably had no experience with managing money. He was only interested in the pleasures of sin for a season. But that pleasure was only temporary and it soon came to an end. There must've been a day when he looked into his money pouch and found it empty.

We've often supposed that those who shared in his sinful ways became hardhearted and refused to take care of him once his money was gone. That may or may not be the case. We're told that there was a famine that swept over the land where he had gone and so I am sure that all of his party going friends were suffering just as much as he was.

Can you picture what it would've been like for this penniless young man to begin a job search! He had no experience and certainly no talent for managing money. The only thing that became available to this Jewish boy was tending a man's hog farm operation. How degrading it must've been to him, raising animals that were "unclean" to the Jewish people. Not only that there was no pay involved. His only wages came from eating that disgusting food he fed to pigs!

As the young man's stomach growled louder and louder his heart grew softer and softer. His thoughts went back to his father's home and how well his father treated his servants. He decided to return to his father and asked for a position as a servant since he did not deserve to be a son any longer. Wow! What a transformation of his heart! And so his journey began and I'm sure with each step he was praying that his father would hire him even though he did not deserve it.

It was while he was far away from the family home that the father saw the familiar figure of his son. He could not wait for his son to come all the way to him, but he ran to meet that wayward son. While the son tried to repeat his memorized speech, his father welcomed him into his arms.

Orders were given and the returning son was clothed in splendor. A feast was prepared, friends invited, and rejoicing began. The one who was lost was home at last!

But someone was missing. The older brother with the bitter attitude was not part of the rejoicing. He had been out in the fields. It seems to imply that he did not trust others and so he tried to do everything himself. As he drew close to the house he heard the sound of laughter and rejoicing. When he was told his brother had returned he became even more bitter, angry, and resentful. He refused to enter the house!

Just as the father rushed to welcome his young son, he rushed to the side of his older son. He begged him to come in and be a part of the celebration, but the older brother refused.

What a lesson we learned from this parable. It is possible to become a prodigal son or daughter without leaving home. Our churches are full of prodigal children. They go through the motions of being a faithful child of the King, but in their hearts they hold bitterness and resentment along with many other secret sins.

As you once again recall this poignant parable, where do you see yourself? Both sons were lost but only one returned to the father. I hope you will be that one!

SAUL'S DRAMATIC CHANGE

To say that Saul was dedicated and committed would be an understatement. His life was committed to God and he was following the narrow road of a Pharisee.

He was sincere and yet we know that he was sincerely wrong. Studying at the feet of the most popular Pharisees of his day he was learning, but he was being taught bitterness, anger, and bigotry. His one aim was to stamp out the growing number of disciples of Jesus Christ. His very name brought fear among the Christian community all through the Middle East.

Damascus was a city roughly 135 miles northeast of Jerusalem. Why Saul felt it was necessary to go to that particular city to arrest believers we are not told. It would certainly seem that there are more believers nearer to Jerusalem. I personally think that God had a hand in directing his thoughts to this particular city.

Today that distance can be traveled in less than an hour by plane or a few hours in a car. In Saul's day the journey would've taken something like two weeks. That would not be an easy task.

Where do you suppose Saul had intended to stay when he arrived in Damascus? I have no idea and we are not told. My personal supposition is that he intended to secure lodging in some public inn located in Damascus. As it would turn out, that particular location would be on Straight Street.

We are not told the number of companions that were traveling with Saul or anything about them. Since his authority from the High Priest was to arrest believers and return them to Jerusalem, my thought is that his companions may have been Temple soldiers. At least they would have been prepared to guard any believers that were to be returned to Jerusalem.

Just outside of Damascus things changed radically for Saul and possibly the others. A brilliant light suddenly surrounded Saul and his companions. Saul fell to the ground and suddenly found himself in the presence of Jesus the Messiah!

When you come into the presence of Jesus things change. This should give hope and confidence to any of us who have family or loved ones who are unbelievers. In one moment of time Saul changed from a persecutor of Jesus to his faithful follower.

If we were to look over Saul's shoulder, actually he was flat on the ground, but if we could catch a glimpse of those men who were with him, we would see terror on their faces. They saw the light, they heard the sound, but they saw no one! But they knew something significant had happened.

When the light disappeared and Saul struggled to his feet he was totally blind. He groped around in the blackness until one of the men touched him and offered to lead him the rest of the way.

Here is where the story leaves many unanswered questions. Who made the arrangements for the temporary living quarters while they were in Damascus? Saul was in no condition to make decisions, therefore it must have been one of the men who was traveling with him.

It is at this point I wonder about the facilities where they stayed. Was it a place where followers of Jesus felt comfortable, or was it a place where the enemies of Jesus were welcome? Perhaps we will never know until we get to heaven.

At this location on Straight Street, Saul spent the next three days praying and fasting. We are told that he neither ate nor drank for all of that time. It must have been an intimate time with the Lord. One thing we are told is that the Lord told him a man by the name of Ananias would come and touch him and he would receive his sight.

The Lord is faithful and true! He appeared to Ananias and gave him the orders to go to Straight Street. At first Ananias tried to explain to God what type of man Saul was. Isn't that very much like we are today? God tells us to do something and we presume to know more than he does. God forgive us! Ananias swallowed his fear, proceeded to that place on Straight Street where his presumed adversary was waiting to be healed. Ananias obeyed, touched Saul with hands of faith and Saul received his sight!

I think there's more to the story than we really have been told. It's not that the writer of the book of Acts wants to keep us in the dark, but evidently it is just not something that we need to know specifically. The unexplained portion of this story is what about the men that were with Saul? When they left Jerusalem were they the enemies of the cross? Did they have the same resentment as Saul did toward believers?

Here is the Pastor Cecil opinion. These men were strong enough to assist Saul in arresting the believers in Damascus. That means when Ananias came into the place were Saul was it was fairly certain that his companions would still be there. They would have been strong enough to overpower Ananias with no difficulty whatsoever.

With that in mind I feel certain that these men became believers themselves. They might have become believers back on the road when the Lord Jesus met Saul, or when Ananias appeared and placed healing hands on his former enemy. That is one of the questions I would like to ask them when I meet them in heaven.

I want to leave us all with the thought that perhaps the enemies of the cross could very easily become our brothers and sisters in the Lord. We must not rush to judgment without leaving room for the work of the Holy Spirit to transform lives!

WEARINESS

Do you ever get weary of hearing people complain about how weary they are? I sometimes feel like saying; "I'm sick and tired of hearing you talk about how you are sick and tired!" Being the sweet and gentle person that I am, I am able to restrain myself. I can hear those who know me laughing right now....Please stop!

It seems as though weariness has been with us for a very long time. After the sin of Adam and Eve in the garden, the judgment that came from God to our first ancestors was that from that moment on they had to work and labor and experience weariness.

Before the age of labor saving devices, hard work exceeded anything that many of us can even imagine in our modern society. We have grown weak and anemic when it comes to work.

There have been programs created by television promoters to take individuals or families into a wilderness type setting and allow them to live the way people did one or two hundred years ago. You can observe as they reach their limit of endurance and are not able to follow what had been commonplace back then.

I've tried to figure out why it was so difficult and then I thought of my high school days playing football. Before the season began workouts were established. We had sore muscles we had forgotten even existed. I can remember coming home after practice late in the evening wondering if it was worth it all. After several weeks muscles began to be developed, stamina increased and weariness was greatly reduced.

There is more to weariness than simply physical conditioning. Mental weariness perhaps is even more prevalent than physical weariness. Mental fatigue is totally exhausting. I have heard students complaining in the last several years about how difficult it was to study and go to class. It reminded me of my college days when I was working full-time (forty-eight hours a week) and taking a full college load of 18 semester hours. It gave me a whole new meaning of weariness!

Focusing our attention on this picture of weariness, is there anything we can do? By that I mean can we actually overcome weariness? I think we can. The answer is very clearly revealed in God's word. One of the first passages I ever memorized in Scripture was **Isaiah 40:30-31;** *"Even the youths shall faint and be weary, and the young men shall utterly fall, but those who wait on the LORD shall renew their strength; they shall mount up with wings like eagles, they shall run and not be weary, they shall walk and not faint."*

The passage of Scripture came to mean more to me following the death of our oldest daughter, Brenda in July 1991. I knew she had been working on a belated birthday present for me, and shortly before she died she presented a counted cross stitch with a bald Eagle and the words from this passage of Scripture in Isaiah chapter 40.

People have tried to deal with weariness by sleep, recreation, vacation, or all sorts of entertainment. In most cases they end up being more exhausted after all of their supposedly relaxing activities than before. So what is the spiritual answer to weariness? Well the answer is given very plainly in this passage when it says that we are to wait on the Lord. Just what does that mean? Well it means we should cool our Jets, as it were, and instead of running ahead of God and then wanting him to give us rest, we are to rest in the knowledge that he knows what is best and his timing is always perfect.

Even the youths shall faint and be weary, And the young men shall utterly fall, But those who wait on the Lord Shall renew their strength; They shall mount up with wings like eagles, They shall run and not be weary, They shall walk and not faint.

(Isaiah 40:30-31)

COMPROMISE!

It is safe to say that it is far easier to see the sand in others than in ourselves. Since our first parents, Adam and Eve, yielded to the temptation of the serpent back in the garden, sin has been passed down to each and every person who has ever lived. That in no way excuses us, but it certainly does explain to us that sin is constantly our enemy.

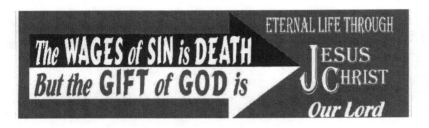

What is the result of sin? The immediate answer is death! I want to say that again sin leads to death. Stop and think of the number of people that we have known, perhaps even ourselves who have witnessed the devastation and death brought about by sin. Sin never leads to a positive outcome but to death. Twice in Ezekiel chapter 18 we are told that the soul that sins must surely die!

Sampson was a very interesting character that we are introduced to in the 13th chapter of the book of Judges. He was unbelievably strong physically, but equally weak morally and spiritually. I think this was significant since Israel was weak morally and spiritually.

Because the people of Israel had turned their back on God they had endured domination by the Philistines for forty years. Then God revealed to a couple that this formerly barren woman bear a son. She was not to use strong drink of any kind and the prophesied son was to be raised as a Nazarite. That meant he was never to use strong drink nor was his hair ever to be cut.

The woman faithfully obeyed the angel's instructions and she delivered a strong young son who was named Sampson. The parents faithfully raised him to be separate and set apart as a Nazarite. However there was something lacking in his character. He was self-absorbed and failed to recognize his calling.

Even though the Philistines were the enemies and oppressors of Israel, Sampson spent more time associating with them than with his own people. It is a sad picture of human weakness as we observe Sampson and Delilah.

He should have been wise enough to discern that she was not interested in his welfare as much as for her own agenda. Compromise followed compromise as Delilah made every effort possible to discover the secret of his strength. It is interesting to note that each time he supposedly told her his secret, it had to do with his hair.

As we read the pages of Judges 13 and beyond, it seems impossible for Sampson not to realize that this woman was seeking to destroy him. Time after time he would fall asleep with his head on her lap only to have her cry out that his enemies were upon him. Just as often she realized that he had deceived her and not told her the truth.

He finally tired of the game that she was playing and so he finally told her the truth that the secret of his strength was in his long hair. If his hair was cut he would have no more strength than a common man. You know what was coming!

When Delilah called that his enemies were upon him Sampson awoke presuming that his strength was still there, but it was gone. He had become so lulled into compromising that he failed to maintain his guard.

It was a tragic picture of this once mighty man now being led away with no strength at all. His eyes were painfully gouged out and he was led away to work as a slave on a grist mill.

But God is gracious and his love endures far longer than man's faithfulness! As the years passed Sampson's hair grew once again and his strength returned. The end of his life came when supernaturally it pushed upon the pillars of the huge arena where his enemies had gathered and they were suddenly destroyed. God had used him in spite of his past failures!

Many times we are very much like Sampson. By that I mean that we spend far too much time with the enemy and far too little time doing the work that God desires for us to do. Compromise is a word that has been used as a complement but so very often it leads to death.

Think back up on your own life and the time when you felt conviction about something and kept clear of it. Then little by little you began to chip away at the foundation stone of your faith.

Each person is different and there is no way to explain exactly what that compromise is. But one thing I do know is that when we feel the Holy Spirit convicting us of something we had better be very careful and stay clear of it.

I once heard a brilliant minister explain how frequently we are led astray, the illustration was that a person prays to be allowed to do something and the Holy Spirit says; **"NO!"** Sometime later we come to the Lord in prayer and ask for God's approval and the Holy Spirit says; "No!" We wait for a period of time and again seek God's approval for the very same thing and the Holy Spirit says; "No."

I think you may see where this is heading, but let me continue anyway. After a period of time we come back to the Lord seeking His approval. This time there was only silence. With great joy we feel like we are free to do that since the Lord has not said it is wrong.

What is wrong with this illustration? The answer is very clear the Holy Spirit has not changed, it is our hearing that has changed. More precisely it's our discernment of the will of God for our life's that has changed.

Now is the time to prayerfully look deep within our heart. Are we closer to God or closer to the world? Are the things of eternal value occupying the majority of our time or the things of the world?

JUMPIN' JEHOSHAPHAT

You may have heard or even used the expression "Jumpin' Jehoshaphat!" without having any knowledge of what the name means.

In II Chronicles 18 we read that he was a king in the southern kingdom of Judah. Unlike many of the other kings in Judah he did what was right in the eyes of the Lord. When I say he was unlike many of the other kings, I think it is important to review what the kings of Israel and Judah were like.

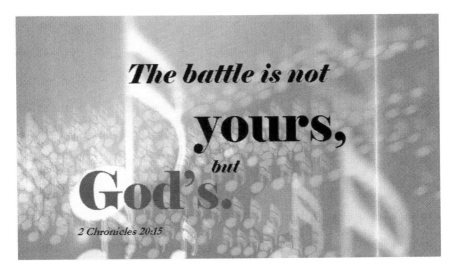

In the northern kingdom of Israel there were a total of 19 kings before they were taken into captivity by the Assyrians. All of them were characterized as being evil kings. How sad that they had turned their back on the God who had delivered them and prepared the land for them. In the southern kingdom of Judah there were a total of 20 kings before they were taken into captivity by the Babylonians. Of this number eight of them were either characterized as being godly or somewhat godly. The other 12 were just as evil as the kings in the northern kingdom.

Jehoshaphat's father Asa was a good and godly king and his son followed his example. After fortifying his country against an attack from Israel he married into the very family of evil King Ahab of Israel. You would think that such divine blessings would insure that he would continue to be faithful to the Lord.

This ungodly alliance was the only flaw that I can detect in reading the account of Jehoshaphat. He agreed to go with Ahab into battle that cost Ahab his life, and almost cost him his life as well. He quickly *jumped* back to Judah where God blessed him. We are told that the fear of the Lord fell on the kingdoms surrounding Judah and they were afraid to make war against Jehoshaphat.

Let me take an opportunity here to express how easy it is for us to forget who our enemy is. We can never compromise with evil in any shape or form. To associate with those who fail to honor the truth of God's word will inevitably lead to danger. The godly standards that once had been important to us can easily slip and slide away. Giving a little here and a little there will ultimately result in us being far from God and the true people of God.

Jumpin' Jehoshaphat was blessed of God and enjoyed peace for many years. It was during this time that he sent priests all around the kingdom to instruct the people in the ways of God. It was a time of revival and the people found themselves blessed of God more than they could ever remember.

It was in the midst of this spiritual revival that a threat arose from three nations: the people of Ammon, Moab, and Mount Seir. It was such a massive force that, defeat seemed to be inevitable.

What do you do when you're surrounded by forces that are sure to overwhelm you? I hope you will do as Jehoshaphat did. He cried out to the Lord his God and laid the matter before Him. You see the battle was not Jehoshaphat's, it was the Lord's. It is the same way for us today. Regardless of the circumstances, we serve a God who is abundantly able to do even more than we can ever ask or think!

Then Jehoshaphat's people marched out to meet the enemy. They did not rely on battle formations, but on praise and celebration to the Lord. The priest led the people in singing praises to God. I can almost visualize Jehoshaphat leaping with praise to his God who had never failed him.

As the enemy stretched out before them, something extremely unusual happened. God stepped in and fought the battle! The people of Ammon began to attack the people of Moab, then the people of Mount Seir. The devastation was complete, the entire enemy force destroyed each other and no one was left. I can almost see Jehoshaphat jumping up and down in praise to the God who had delivered His people.

We need to take heart from the lessons we read about the lives of these real life characters in the Old Testament. They were tempted to stray away from God just as much as we are today. Every time they did they had to suffer the consequences.

Anytime we stray away from the Word of God and his will for our life, we are likely to experience loss in our life. We may not be able to measure it in dollars and cents, but we certainly will experience it in our contentment and peace of mind.

Are you experiencing heavy a cloud over you at this moment? When was the last time you jumped for joy in the presence of the Lord? By that I do not mean a show in some congregation for everybody else's jumping and carrying on, but that delight that overwhelms when we know we are placing God on the throne of our life.

Pray with me right now please: *"Lord Jesus I have placed you on the back burner of my life. I have chosen to make other things more important than my relationship with You. I have spoken words with my mouth but have not lived in the manner that I know you want me to live. Lord we have failed you. We have allowed the things in the sins of the world to creep into our midst until they become a part and parcel of our life. Please forgive us, please heal our families, our communities, our nation. Fight the battles that only You can find and might we be prepared ahead of time to praise You and give You glory, and we pray this in Jesus precious name amen"*

Let us consider what happened:

- 2 Chronicles 18:1, "by marriage he allied himself with Ahab."
- 2 Chronicles 18:2-4, "I am as you are, and my people as your people; we will be with you in the war." "Please inquire for the word of the Lord today."

GET IN STEP!

Twice in my life I have been in military training situations. The first time was when basic training back in 1953. I had enlisted in the United States Air Force and was stationed at Parks Air Force Base in California. For anyone entering the military it is a cultural shock!

Individuals became a unit! Your hair was cut the same way (it was shaved off!). You would enter the processing building wearing civilian clothes with hairstyles wide-ranging from neatly cut to long and shaggy. You exited the building with exactly the same haircuts and uniforms that were identical. Things were-a changing in your little world!

The other significant change was you did not walk anywhere! You marched everywhere you went and you went as a group. In the Air Force we were assigned to a Squadron which was composed of several Flights. That was over 60 years ago, but to my best recollection we had about 100 men in our flight. I think there were 10 flights in our squadron. With 1000 men marching to and fro it was quite a sight!

We were consistently practicing marching on the parade ground. That was different than marching to and from the multiple activities of basic training. The parade ground was the showpiece of the entire squadron, if not the entire base.

It was a fantastic site to see over 1000 servicemen marching as one man. A military band is playing and each Airman marched in rhythm to the drum. From the reviewing stand seeing all of the legs moving in unison was a sight to behold!

As each flight approached the reviewing stand the Sgt. who was commanding the flight gave brisk orders. At just the right moment as he was approaching the reviewing officers, he commanded; Eyes Right! Each column except the one on the far right there's the stand with snap their heads 45° toward the stand and wait for his command; Hand Salute! We would hold our salute until we had passed the stand and heard the command; Ready Front!

That same scenario was played out years later in 1963 when I was in Officers Training School (OTS). There was a big difference on our final parade. In basic training we were awarded one stripe signifying Airman Third Class. After (OTS) we received a gold bar signifying Second Lieutenant. We were now commissioned officers!

As we travel through life is important to remember that we are not just living for ourselves. We need to keep in step with the God ordained plan for our life. It all starts when we confess our sins and invite Jesus Christ into our heart to become the Lord of our life-our Commanding Officer!

There are many Christians who are out of step with what God desires for their life. They might go to an altar and pray a prayer inviting the Lord into their life, but nothing changes. They stumble along spiritually and from all outward appearances there has been no change in their behavior.

I clearly remember seeing basic training members emerging from the Processing Center looking and acting differently. They were no longer undisciplined men and women of the civilian world, but they marched to the beat of a different drummer. That needs to be the case spiritually!

The second assignment as a commissioned officer was at an in Shreveport, Louisiana. Throughout the day the men and women who were enlisting in one of the branches of the military would be processed, given a physical examination and filling out page after page of information. Their final process of the day was to be formally sworn in to the military. That was the task which had been assigned to me. I would say something like this: "Raise your right hand and repeat after me: I (state your full name) do solemnly swear to support and defend the Constitution of the United States against all her enemies, foreign and domestic. So help me God."

From the moment I administered that oath of office these men and women were no longer free to do as they saw fit. They were now subject to the orders that were given by their superiors. They would be told when to eat, went to sleep, when to exercise, when to attend classes, and when to do those things that would shape and form them into defenders of the United States. I'm sure other nations have similar oaths of office for those who entered the service of their country.

The Apostle Paul was not a soldier, but he knew what was expected of a soldier. Read what he wrote in Second Timothy 2:1-4; *"You therefore, my son, be strong in the grace that is in Christ Jesus. And the things that you have heard from me among many witnesses, commit these to faithful men who will be able to teach others also. You therefore must endure hardship as a good soldier of Jesus Christ. No one engaged in warfare entangles himself with the affairs of this life, that he may please him who enlisted him as a soldier."*

Wow! What powerful words! It reveals to me that we are in a battle against a force that threatens each and every person that is born. From that long ago time in the Garden of Eden when Adam and Eve sinned, a battle has raged. Each soul has been born requiring a Savior who would rescue them. It is a battleground!

The question that arises is which army are we going to be enlisted in? By birth we are a member of Satan's army. To join God's army requires a new birth. The stakes are high. Our eternal destiny is on the line. Not only our destiny, but the destiny of those who are around us. When we get in step with God we are part of his mighty army to save as many souls as possible.

I would like to administer the oath of office to you right now if you have never enlisted in God's army. "I (state your full name) do solemnly confess that I am a sinner and need Jesus Christ to be my Savior. I solemnly swear that I will serve Him and March in step with his directions. So help me God."

WHAT IF---?!

WHAT IF THERE IS NO GOD:

If you look at the title for this chapter, you may think that I have lost my mind! That may be the case but there some things I like to share from my heart. Things I have been meditating on perhaps for a good part of my life.

IF THERE IS NO GOD, EVERYTHING IS PERMITTED.

Across the years of my life I've had an opportunity to share the gospel of Jesus Christ with many people. Some have been eager to receive the good news of the gospel and have opened their heart and receive Jesus Christ as their personal Savior. Others have rejected every witness that I have made.

Now I understand that there is no way that you can argue a person into believing faith. It must be a free choice. My heart has been broken over and over by those who firmly rejected Christ.

Over the years I have read histories of noted atheists who mocked and jeered those who believed in Jesus.

But in the last moments of their life, as eternity stretched out before them, their demeanor changed radically and they open their heart to receive Jesus Christ as their personal Savior.

Occasionally I have observed this in my own experience. I can recall one incident where a man had steadfastly denied God throughout his entire life. His wife and daughter were committed Christians and had consistently witnessed to him without result. He was in his 70's and his wife was very ill in a Convalescent Center. I am not sure what prompted it, but he called and wanted to meet with me and said he was ready to give his heart to the Lord.

What a joy it was to go through the plan of salvation and pray with him as he opened his heart and received Jesus Christ as his personal Savior. I asked him if he would like to go to the Convalescent Center and share the Lord's Supper with his wife. He had never before participated in a Communion Celebration. It was one of the sweetest and most precious times as I served the two and prayed with them. Only a few days later this man suffered a stroke and died soon after.

We never know exactly how long we will have the ability to choose our eternal destiny. To me it is one of the greatest gambles that a person can ever make to deny the existence of God and the necessity of a new birth.

For the sake of argument let us suppose that there is no hereafter. I do not believe that in a moment, but let's suppose that that is the case. The most happy, contented, and joyful people I have ever known are Christians. They have a love for God and a love for others.

In the darkest hours of pain and suffering they have hope and rejoicing. Their hearts are full of anticipation of what lies ahead. They are contented! That does not mean that they are free of trials and tribulations. But it does mean that they face these obstacles by looking at what lies ahead for them. I am one of those people! Even if there were no hereafter I am satisfied and contented. It has been a beautiful satisfying life and I have no regrets.

Those doubters who hold to the idea that there is no God and that when we die we simply go back to the dust from which we came are basically miserable. They have a negative attitude toward most things on earth and seldom do they find contentment. Always searching but never achieving the peace that passes all understanding. What an empty way to exist!

If there is no God and there is no heaven or hell, the believer still wins. The love, joy, and peace that floods their soul is far better than the cynical doubt and bitterness of the unbeliever.

WHAT IF THERE IS A GOD?

Here is where the "rubber meets the road" so to speak. All the bravado of the cynical doubter suddenly is faced with the reality that they have made an eternal error. There is no second chance to rectify a wrong decision. Let me emphasize that with a parable that Jesus taught.

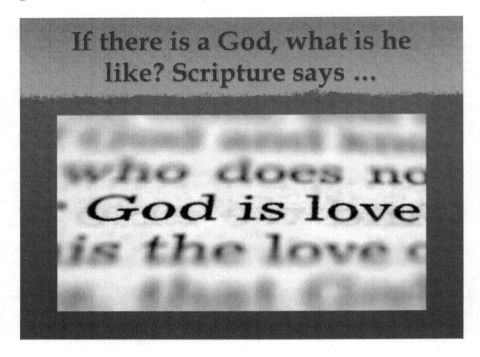

If there is a God, what is he like? Scripture says ...

God is love

The Rich Man and Lazarus
Luke 16:19-31

"There was a certain rich man who was clothed in purple and fine linen and fared sumptuously every day. But there was a certain beggar named Lazarus, full of sores, who was laid at his gate, desiring to be fed with the crumbs which fell from the rich man's table. Moreover the dogs came and licked his sores. So it was that the beggar died, and was carried by the angels to Abraham's bosom. The rich man also died and was buried. And being in torments in

Hades, he lifted up his eyes and saw Abraham afar off and Lazarus in his bosom. Then he cried and said, 'Father Abraham, have mercy on me, and send Lazarus that he may dip the tip of his finger in water and cool my tongue; for I am tormented in this flame.' But Abraham said, 'Son, remember that in your lifetime you received your good things, and likewise Lazarus evil things; but now he is comforted and you are tormented. And besides all this, between us and you there is a great gulf fixed, so that those who want to pass from here to you cannot, nor can those from there pass to us.' Then he said, 'I beg you therefore, father, that you would send him to my father's house, for I have five brothers that he may testify to them, lest they also come to this place of torment.' Abraham said to him, 'They have Moses and the prophets; let them hear them.' And he said, 'No, father Abraham; but if one goes to them from the dead, they will repent.' But he said to him, 'If they do not hear Moses and the prophets, neither will they be persuaded though one rise from the dead.'"

I am always struck by the difference that occurs when each man dies. Lazarus dies and is carried by the angels to a paradise with God. The rich man died and they took him out and buried him. How empty and how sad!

There is an eternity stretching out before us and the decisions we make now will determine where we will spend that eternity! You can mock, smirk, or have a condescending attitude toward the realities that I have just shared. But one second after your eyes closed in death you will know your eternal destiny. My prayer is that I will see you inside the gates of glory!

The Parable of the

RICH MAN
& LAZARUS

LUKE 16:19-31

THE SAUL BEFORE PAUL

Pride is a devastating thing! Almost every day we are exposed to people who at one time were common and approachable. They had pleasant personalities and never thought more highly of themselves than they should.

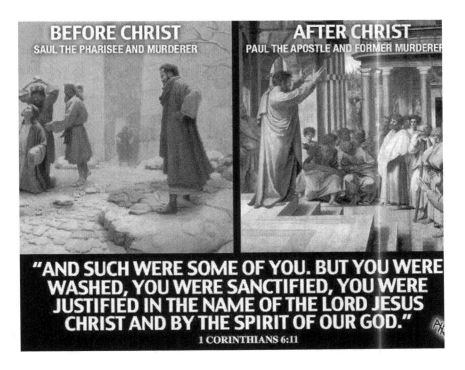

"AND SUCH WERE SOME OF YOU. BUT YOU WERE WASHED, YOU WERE SANCTIFIED, YOU WERE JUSTIFIED IN THE NAME OF THE LORD JESUS CHRIST AND BY THE SPIRIT OF OUR GOD."
1 CORINTHIANS 6:11

But then something happened. These same individuals began to receive praise and promotion. When at the outset they were humble minded, after receiving the praise of those around them, they began to act as though they were something special.

In the Old Testament we read about a man who started out humble but before long became a tyrant.

His name was Saul and he was the first King of Israel. He was so humble that at his coronation he hid himself.

If he would've continued with that view of himself throughout his reign things would've been much different. But that was not to be. He considered himself above the law of God and the people. Things had to go his way or heads would roll.

Saul was a tall and imposing figure and from every indication he was the right man to serve as the first king of Israel. The exalted position began to cause Saul to exalt himself.

God gave him an opportunity to make amends and become the man that he should have been, but Saul refused to bow down even before God. The result was a life that was soon to spin out of control and end in catastrophe.

In the political arena we see men and women who are elected to offices and soon begin to strut like a peacock. They may have started as a voice of the people, but once in office they became aloof to the very ones who elected them to office.

It is tragic that we see the same type of behavior in churches. Church leaders begin to show a superior attitude toward the people they are to serve. Instead of being Christ-like they pattern themselves after the world. Their extravagant lifestyle is contrary to the life that Jesus lived while He was here on earth.

We are often tempted to think that this exists only with high-powered individuals. That is not the case. People·can develop a superior attitude even when they are filling a minor position.

If at any time praise is reflected our way, I think it is important that we remember Saul the King. Immediately we should recall Saul who became Paul the Apostle. If ever there was a man who could receive praise it was Paul the Apostle. His letters make up a significant portion of the New Testament, yet he was humble and never exalted himself above others. He was God's man first and foremost.

 I think it is very important that we reflect any compliments or praise to the Lord rather than receiving it our self. Any time we are praised for what we have done we should respond: "TO GOD BE THE GLORY!"

PAUL GETS HIS VISION BACK

WHO ARE YOU TALKING TO?

I am amazed and stunned at the humorous incidents that I find in Scripture. We often read through the Bible without stopping to realize that God certainly does have a sense of humor in getting the message across to the readers.

If I were to ask you the last time you read the book of Numbers, I'm sure that most would answer I do not want to spend my time reading the list genealogies? If that is what you have in your mind concerning the book of Numbers you are very sadly mistaken.

Let me direct your attention to chapter 22 in the book of Numbers. This is the story of Balak and Balaam. Balak was the king of the Moabites. As the children of Israel were making their way from Egypt to the promise land, Balak knew that God had given them victory over their enemies all along the way.

He sent distinguished messengers some 400 miles away to an area near the Euphrates River. They were searching for a diviner named Balaam. They offered a substantial reward for him to come and curse the children of Israel.

It is difficult to know his relationship with God, but he refused to return with the men until he had consulted the Lord. The message he received was that he was not to go with these men. That was the end of the matter and he complied.

Four hundred miles back to Moab with no diviner! I am sure the messengers went with great dread as they reported to Balak. He was furious and sent even higher ranking princes and dignitaries and with even more money to persuade Balaam to come and place a curse on the children of Israel. Back 400 hot and grueling miles they traveled to speak with Balaam once again.

Now since God had told him before he was not to go with them, Balaam should have known what God would say. God is the same yesterday, today and forever! When He says no He means no! But Balaam went to God once again with the same request. This time God told him to go ahead and go with them, but to speak only what He would tell him.

The next morning Balaam got up and saddled his donkey for the arduous trip across the miles to Moab. This is where it gets interesting! God had told Balaam to go with the princes but when he started out it says that God was very angry with him. Why? It tells me that when God says no, He means **NO!** He is not pleased when we refuse to do what He says.

SHOW ME A SIGN

Missouri is known as the "Show-Me" State. I was stationed in Missouri for a few years when I was in the Air Force. Our family enjoyed seeing much of the "Show-Me" State and discovered it had a lot to show.

There is somewhat of a cynical connotation with the idea of demanding to be shown something before we accept it. It presents a picture of a person standing with folded arms demanding a sign. "Prove it!" "I'll believe it when I see it!" These are just two examples of an attitude that demands a sign.

Man says... Show me
and I'll trust you.

God says... Trust me
and I'll show you.

Psalm 126:6

Consider the concept of love. It is easy to say the words, "I love you." But they are just words without a demonstration of love. In other words there must be a way to show a sign of that love. If we say we love someone and then ignore them, it is hard to equate the words with the emotion of love.

A sign of romantic love is demonstrated by giving freely to the person you love. It means making the time spent together of vital importance. When I first met the girl I would one day marry we were both 14. All through our high school years we were inseparable. We enjoyed each other's company and showed the signs of our love by making being beside each other. As young as we were our parents knew our love was real by the way we treated each other. We were showing a sign!

It is one thing to show something freely, but it is an entirely different matter to demand a sign. To demand a sign carries the connotation of doubt. In other words it is like saying; "you have to show me a sign before I will believe it!"

In the Gospels we read about the ministry of Jesus and the many miracles that He performed. Those who chose to believe Him looked deeper than the miracles and saw the promised Messiah.

Those who were entrenched in religious self-righteousness felt threatened. If they were to place their trust in Jesus it would mean surrendering their own pride and position. Therefore they demanded that He show a sign.

It amazes me that Jesus had been showing sign after sign by the miracles He performed. The sick and afflicted were healed, the multitudes were fed, and sinners forgiven. And yet they demanded a sign. What started my thinking on this topic was not current events or even the life that Jesus experienced, it was thing that had occurred to Moses in the wilderness. Wow! That is really going back a long way.

Let me refresh your mind about the incident. Moses had been raised by Pharaoh's daughter and spent 40 years in luxury. It was then he decided to visit his own people, the Israelites. He saw an Egyptian taskmaster beating an Israelite. He came to the man's aid and killed the Egyptian.

The next day as he visited the Israelites, he saw two of them fighting. When he broke the fight up one of them mentioned that they had seen him killed the Egyptian. Immediately he knew that the matter would be known in Pharaoh's household so he fled to Midian.

Moses spent the next 40 years as a shepherd for his father-in-law. The life of a shepherd is isolated and lonely. One day as he was caring for his sheep he noticed a fantastic thing a bush was burning but it was not consumed. In my mind's eye it would be something like a natural gas flame.

As Moses drew near to the burning bush a voice came to him that he was to remove his sandals for this was holy ground. Picture this 80-year-old man who had spent the last 40 years caring for sheep and now seeing this magnificent sight.

I am sure that for 40 years Moses felt like he was a complete failure. His intent was to stand up for his people but he ended up as a failure in his own eyes. But God had different plans for Moses. He was to return to Egypt and lead his people to the promise land.

God gave Moses a sign. I feel that for the most part it has been overlooked by many people. When Moses returned and stood before Pharaoh he was able to throw his staff to the ground and it became a serpent. When he picked it up it became a staff again. He put his hand into his robe and when it came out it was leprous. When he put it back in and removed it is skin had returned to normal.

If we fast-forward we see plague after plague upon Egypt that did not affect the Israelites, as they were protected by God. God gave the order for Passover in which the firstborn of man and beast that was not protected by the blood died.

God so change the hearts of the people of Egypt that they gave gold and precious items to the Israelites who had been slaves prior to this. But that was not the sign that God had promised to Moses.

God provided a pillar of cloud by day and a pillar of fire by night to lead and protect the children of Israel, but that was not the sign. The Red Sea parted and the children of Israel went to crossed on dry ground but when the Egyptian army pursued them the sea closed in upon them and they were all destroyed, but that was not the sign.

Think of all the miracles that took place in the early part of the Exodus. It was a miraculous time and could only be explained by the tender care of God. But none of these miracles was the sign had been promised to Moses.

The sign is found in Exodus 12:3; ***"So He said, 'I will certainly be with you. And there is the sign you shall serve God on this mountain.'"***

This is the sign! Not the miracles, not the deliverance, not the provision, not the plundering of the wealth of Egypt, it was that Moses would return and serve God on this mountain.

I don't think I've ever heard preachers or Bible teachers emphasize this beautiful truth. Sometimes we look for the flashy glittering things and think this is the way God speaks to us and the sign that is given. If God gave a sign to Moses that He was with him when he returned to serve God on the mountain, I think God still gives us that signed today. He wants us to worship him in spirit and in truth.

Instead of searching for miracles and things that would profit from the worlds point of view, come to the mountain of the Lord and worship in spirit and in truth. His promise is that He will be with us. Thank you Lord!

And God said unto Moses, **I AM THAT I AM:** and He said, Thus shalt thou say unto the children of Israel, **I AM hath sent me unto you**

FLOATING ABOVE THE FLOOD

A CLOSER LOOK AT NOAH

I recently was watching a live television feed of attempts to rescue a man who was trapped in floodwaters. He was holding tightly to a telephone pole; but as the minutes turned to hours his stamina began to slip away and he was in danger of being swept to his death. In dramatic fashion rescue boats arrived just in time to save the man's life.

Sometimes the storms of life swirl around us in dramatic fashion. Areas of the world that have never experienced much rain suddenly are hit with a deluge. People scramble for their very lives as the flood waters rise. Vivid scenes show people first on the top of houses, cars, or anything else that will keep them above the flood waters that threaten them.

Perhaps the most dangerous type of flood is a flash flood. When waters rise slowly people have an opportunity to escape. In a flash flood many times the flood is upon them before they have an opportunity to escape.

Even though flash floods may occur suddenly, there are often times when warnings have been issued. Certain areas are prone to flash flooding and warning signs are posted explaining the danger of flash floods in that particular area. The inexperienced person may feel there safe because there is no rain where they are. Even when there is no rain where they are there may be a storm quite some distance away. Flood waters funnel down upon them without warning. **It is always well to observe the caution signs!**

When we think of the flood most often we think of Noah in the book of Genesis. It has been estimated that there were millions of people on the earth at the time of Noah. Yet only Noah, his wife, his three sons, and their wives were the only people who were righteous in God's sight and escaped the flood.

I think it's a lesson to us that those who are righteous will always be in the minority. We wish that there would be more that would respond to the message of the gospel, but we always seem to experience more rejections than those who accept Christ.

If you recall stories about the flood, you will often find distortions. It is amazing that we have based more of our understanding of biblical accounts from novels or some Hollywood misrepresentation than on the Bible. It is questionable whether the people who portray biblical accounts actually have spent the time reading the Bible at all.

You might ask the question, "What does it really matter, just so long as the story is based upon some phase of Scripture?" The answer to that question is very simple. Do we want to listen to what God has to say or what some writer says? For one I would rather listen to what God has to say!

For just a moment let us consider a few things that the Bible has to say about Noah and the flood. The first question that arises is how long did it take for Noah and his sons to build the ark? Nothing is given specifically to determine how long it took. Some have used Genesis 6:3 as the length of time; *"And the LORD said, 'My Spirit shall not strive with man forever, for he is indeed flesh; yet his days shall be one hundred and twenty years.'"* Whether that is actually the time it took the actual construction time is not specifically given.

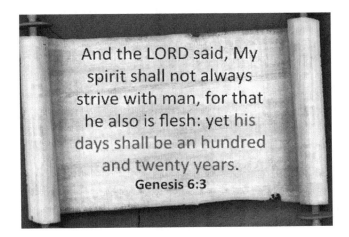

And the LORD said, My spirit shall not always strive with man, for that he also is flesh: yet his days shall be an hundred and twenty years.
Genesis 6:3

Another representation of novelists and filmmakers are the crowds surrounding Noah and his sons as they build the ark. In Scripture there is no such indication. It is very possible that God protected Noah and his sons in such a way that constructed the ark in isolation. I am sure that God provided sufficient building materials and He was also able to insure there was no hindrance from mocking or angry crowds. We also do not read of crowds surrounding the ark demanding to be saved from the floodwaters.

Another common error is that there were only two of each species to be loaded onto the ark. In chapter 6, God tells Noah that he is to take two of each creature into the ark. In chapter 7 however, we read that God tells Noah to take seven of each clean animal and seven of each of the birds of the air. Noah is also instructed to take sufficient food for the animals and for himself and his family. (When we study hibernation habits of certain animals, it is possible that God caused some of the animals to sleep most of the time they were aboard the ark and thus did not require feeding).

It was not necessary for Noah and his sons to search high and wide for the animals to be loaded aboard the ark. When we study the migration patterns of animals we can easily imagine that God placed a magnet within each creature to be loaded into the ark that drew them into a position where they could be saved in order to replenish the earth following the flood. God is good and his mercy extends through all generations!

Moving ahead in the biblical account of the flood, there is considerable speculation as to where the ark came to rest. Modern-day explorers have searched the top of Mount Ararat to find the remains of Noah's Ark. As far as I know there is nothing to substantiate conclusively that the ark has been found. In my own mind I am glad that the ark has **not** been found. I fear that if it were found some people would conceivably make the pieces of the ark objects of worship. God is never pleased for His people to worship man-made objects. He is a jealous God and demands that we worship Him and Him alone!

The Scriptures say that the ark rested on the Mountains of Ararat. To my mind for the ark to come to rest on a mountain peak would not be conducive to replenishing the earth. It is more than likely that the ark rested somewhere near the mountain chain known as the **Mountains of** Ararat, not **Mount** Ararat.

I'm told that almost in every primitive culture there are traditions about the flood that covers the entire Earth. Anthropologists have tried to understand how divergent cultures could come up with such a tradition. To me the answer is very simple. There truly was a flood that covered the entire Earth!

While we may think of water rising creating a flood there are many types of floods. A person may participate in a particular type of behavior that is questionable. At first there's no problem but suddenly they find themselves awash in a flood of their own making.

You may feel that you are experiencing something of a flood in your own life. There is good news my dear friend! If God was able to spare Noah and his family from the devastation of the flood, He is more than able to spare you from the rising waters around you.

The next time you feel the waters of adversity rising around your ankles and up to your kneecaps, look to Jesus and find the ark of salvation that he has prepared for you!

Remember Psalm 30:5; *"For His anger is but for a moment, His favor is for life; Weeping may endure for a night, But joy comes in the morning."*

LOOKING OVER THE WRONG SIDE OF THE FENCE

Psalm 37:1-7
"Do not fret because of evil men or be envious of those who do wrong; for like the grass they will soon wither, like green plants they will soon die away. Trust in the LORD and do good; dwell in the land and enjoy safe pasture. Delight yourself in the LORD and He will give you the desires of your heart. Commit your way to the LORD; trust in Him and He will do this: He will make your righteousness shine like the dawn, the justice of your cause like the noonday sun. Be still before the LORD and wait patiently for Him; do not fret when men succeed in their ways, when they carry out their wicked schemes."

Psalm 37 has been a favorite of mine for many years. In fact the book of Psalms has been a favorite book of mine. It gives us the plans and provisions of the

Lord. Another reason I love it so much is that it is so up to date.

Just look at the words in the passage I have cited above. It is like reading today's newspaper, yet it was written about 3,000 years ago. Evil men were as common then as they are now. David also describes the way we fallen humans are prone to think and act. He lists two worldly reactions: FRET! AND ENVY!

Now consider the way you react when you see the godless, people prosper while the righteous struggle. We FRET! That means we smolder and stew.   This is the hand wringing type of reaction. Some think it is spiritual if we hold our feelings in and try not to let them show. To hold them in is like a spring that is wound too tight and ready to suddenly unwind.

Years ago I heard an illustration about a little boy. (It reminded me of me of my own reactions as a little boy. My problem was that I could not stop talking. My mom said I sometimes almost drove her crazy. I find that hard to believe since I am so quiet now. RIGHT)! Back to the illustration: This little boy was running around and creating such havoc, that his mother made him stop and sit on a foot stool for five minutes. When she pushed him down and he stood back up. She would push back down and again he would stand up. After about three times she told him if he stood up again she would paddle his backside so hard he wouldn't be able to sit down! He finally got the message and at last sat down with his arms folded. He looked up at her and said; *"I may be sitting down on the outside, but I am standing up on the inside!"* That is what we are like when we fret.

The other human reaction is ENVY. We see the bad guys getting all of the neat toys and we pout and get in a snit because they have what we want.
Envy is always a waste of time. The things of this world will all pass away, so why place so much emphasis on them? Someone has done a survey of winners of large sums of money from various lotteries. They asked them this question, *"Were you more content before winning or now?"* It was almost unanimous that they were <u>much</u> more content before winning.

Now comes the good part!! Look at the words I underlined in the passage from Psalm 37. **TRUST, DELIGHT, COMMIT, BE STILL.** This is the pattern that we should set for ourselves to find real peace and contentment. We place our **TRUST** in the trustworthiness of the Lord, knowing that He is the one who is able to protect and lead us. We are to **DELIGHT** in all things. Our joy comes from the Lord and so as we spend time with Him we never have to feel alone. When others leave us, we have Him always beside us.

I remember speaking with a new widow some years ago. I had intended to counsel her, but instead came away walking on air. She told of how the Lord was so close to her when she was alone that it was almost as if God's arms enfolded her. Wow! That is **delighting** in the Lord.

The next step in the pattern is to **COMMIT**. The consistent walk of the believer is not a wishy-washy thing that is up and down. It is a firm covenant that we establish with the Lord. He shed His blood to provide us with our salvation, and we **COMMIT** to ourselves to make Him the Lord of our life. That means He is the Boss. We do not tell Him what to do, but rather we search His Word and discover what His plans are for those who are His very own children.

The last step in the process, is to **BE STILL**. Another way to state this is to **REST**. We do not need to be in a constant state of activity. We simply need to rest in Him completely.

There is no need to look over the fence of ungodly people, wishing for the things of this world. Things of the world never satisfy, and they will all pass away.

We need to spend time studying this passage over and over then start putting it into practice. See what a change it will make in your life. It is worth it! Keep your eyes on your own side of the fence.

A FINAL WORD

We traditionally think of God's Bountiful Blessings during Thanksgiving Celebrations. That is all well and good and I certainly believe we need to set aside special days in which we pause and thank God for all He has blessed us with. In the majority of our times of Thanksgiving we tend to focus our thanks on the material and/or physical blessings. We should!

In this book I have attempted to highlight the spiritual blessings to be found in God's word. In doing so I know that I have barely scratched the surface. There are so many blessings that it seems each time I open my bible I find more and more spiritual gems.

It is my desire that this small book will inspire you to seek out more Bountiful Blessings. When you find them, please make a point of sharing them with others.

May God richly bless you as you bless others by your words and your actions!

Pastor Cecil A. Thompson

PastorCecil.com

THE SANDS OF ETERNITY

NOTES

Made in the USA
San Bernardino, CA
15 June 2016